Poetic reflections of love in life...

An environmentally friendly book printed and bound in England by
www.printondemand-worldwide.com

PEFC Certified
This product is from sustainably managed forests and controlled sources
www.pefc.org

This book is made entirely of chain-of-custody materials

First published 2012 by Fast-Print Publishing of
Peterborough, England.

www.fast-print.net/store.php

A LIFE OF LOVE

ISBN: 978-178035-475-0

A catalogue record for this book is available from the British Library

Contents

Dedication

This book I dedicate to my Father, who gave me the inspiration to write poetry.

I grew up reading his poems that were so meaningful, they inspired me to put my own feelings and emotions into words.

Thank you, Dad.

Acknowledgements

My poetry has carried me through some dark and difficult periods of illness in my life, when I felt fragile and lost. Having belief in myself again, I carried on writing my poetry, which I truly love to do.

It is with the love and support of my precious husband, children and grandchildren that I was able to pull through those testing times and again see a brighter, better future. They have been my inspiration through all of this. Thank you all. I count myself as truly blessed and they are the reason I wake up each day. I am very fortunate to live in a lyrical, musically talented family who write from their hearts and sing from their souls.

My poems are but a small piece of a larger puzzle. All together, I hope we make a beautiful picture.

Many thanks to my family, friends and associates with whom I have had the pleasure of working with. Pam Kounougakis, my special friend, has helped me with information and encouraged me to further my vision to produce a book of my poetry.

I hope this will be a fruitful journey towards achieving my dreams.

Reflections

I have come to realise that I can only do so much,
I cannot live life for others
I haven't got the magic touch.
But yet I do as much as I can,
Whatever I can, whenever I can.
It's a pleasure
I do it with leisure,
It's my gift
From man to man.
My heart that loves purely
Is always willing to give
To hold out a hand
To get one out of trouble
Out of sinking sand.
So if you need me
Don't forget to say,
I'll be close, I'll be near,
Forever and a day.

The Greatest Gift is to Love and Be Loved in Return

To have and to hold.
Health, wealth, love, make the most of it.
Each of us should have the passion to live, love, and be happy.

Growing older with you is a pleasure.
Rising up together, at the break of day, what more can I ask?
Every day is a good day with you by my side.
Always be my friend, my soulmate, in my life.
True love cannot be bought; it has to be felt.
Earth, sun, sky and sea revolve around the love I have for you.
Sunshine of my life you are!
Tender, quiet moments, just knowing that we are in love.

Getting close to you each day. Is it love on the way?
In love and life, I am fulfilled.
Falling in love is magic.
There is no other love than my love for you.

Is it true? That you love me as much as I love you.
Silent messages can be sent through the eyes of love.

Treasure the time we have together.
Only you, do I adore.

Loving you is the greatest pleasure in my life.
Our love will last for ever more.
Value each other, and our love will grow stronger.
Ever in my thoughts.

All that I have is yours to take.
Never leave me lonely.
Do I live in your mind, like you live in mine?

Be mine and I'll be yours forever.
Endless pleasure, in a land we dream of together.

Let me be lost in your love.
On cloud seven when I am with you.
Vows taken in true love should never be broken.
Enjoying time together, whatever the weather.
Dream an endless dream with you.

In my world you are my king and I your queen.
Now and forever, always mine.

Roads to paradise are always open to those who seek.
Ever lovingly, yours, so take my hand.
Tell me that you love me truly.
Under the stars, mystical moonlight, dancing with
you. Paradise!
Return to me, my love wants you only.
Nobody loves you like I do.

Is This Love At First Sight?

Just another day
Get up, get dressed,
Rush, rush, rush,
Lots to do, but
Must not forget
My daily train
I have to catch yet.

This train ride is my regular journey
To get from A to B,
A part of my life, my work,
A part of me.

I look around me on
This regular run,
A quick nod here, a smile there,
To those who have time to spare,
Share the time of day,
In a polite and social way.
Just then,
I gazed around aimlessly,
My gaze wandered to you
And stopped suddenly.
I saw you, and you saw me,
Our eyes met just for a moment,
My heart missed a beat,
Then pounded, so furiously.

You smiled back,
Something happened to me
Out on the railway track.

So tight we were in the crowded train,
But our minds were as one,
Not in a dream, but reality.

My life changed that fateful day.
Since then I can feel,
I have a goal,
I've found my soul,
I've found someone so real.
So hello and goodbye for now,
Till we meet again,
Till then I'll hold on
I'll get by somehow.

Now I know my life has changed,
Since then I have you on my mind,
I wonder if I live in your mind?
Like you live in mine
Au revoir, my love,
See you again,
Until the next time.

Lost and Found

Summertime is always around,
So much fun, sun, warmth,
Laughter to be found.
We are lucky you and I
To see the sun, feel the warm breezes in the sky.
Let's take it all in, now,
Let our happiness begin.
Forget those days; we were caught in a maze,
Our life was not ours, not clear,
In a haze.

We lived for everyone else,
Not thinking of ourselves.
Then summer came, things changed for us,
Somehow we came to life again,
We found something we had lost.
So precious the gift,
So priceless the cost.

We found the precious gift of loving
As man and wife they say,
Our love was strong, so true,
It came through.
It's you for me and me for you,
We are happy, at the end of the day,
Our summertime is here to stay.

Our Treasure

God gave us a handful of precious diamonds,
Together we treasure them,
Gave them our name,
They make us whole,
They are our life and soul,
Our pride and joy we are proud to say,
They are the reason we wake up each day.

They dream a dream, and make it real
They live, and love life,
It's the way they feel.
New dawns, new days, they'll open the door,
The future is theirs, not ours for sure.
Carry on, be strong,
At the end of the day,
You are diamonds, unique,
In your own special way.

True Love

You are my love, my life, my soul,
It's pure love I feel,
It's your love that makes me whole,
It's your love that is so real.
The music of my life is living with you,
The rhythm of my love is giving to you,
The chimes of my heart always sing for you,
The bells of my heart always ring.

My world, my life, my dreams
Are for you only.
Without you, my world would empty
I would be lost,
And lonely.

Togetherness

Smiles on our faces,
Hearts aglow.
Peace on our minds,
Let everyone know.
The dreams we shared,
Days spent together,
Enjoying each other,
Whatever the weather.

Love's sweet memories
We held for a while,
Paradise on Earth,
This was the style.
True colours of life
We lived you and I.
How great was our love?
As big as the sky!

Living and Loving

Together we've gone through thick and thin.
Had ups and downs in life,
We've been tested in life loving,
And living,
As husband and wife.

We've ridden the waves,
Sheltered from the storms.
Through all of this,
You've made sure, my love
I've come to no harm.

My love for you
Has been strong too,
We've played the same game
You for me, and me for you.
So,
I hope for you I've done the same.

The Ebbing of Life

The days are getting shorter now,
The nights are drawing near,
Time spent together matters now
Because there'll be a time
When we're not here.
For us to be without each other
Is a time that I dread,
As togetherness is the bond
That holds us so strong and solid.
With a golden thread.

All That I Have

All that I have is yours to take,
All that you have is yours to make,
My gift to you is my eternal love,
See it, feel it, use it,
Don't abuse it,
Keep it safe,
Treasure it, pleasure it,
Don't refuse it,
It's that love that rules the human race.
Most of all my love, for me,
Never lose it.

A Song In My Heart

There's many a song my heart sings
Every time I think of you
A love bell rings.
Can you hear it, my love?

It is a part of you
And a part of me,
It is of a time we spent together
When we loved, laughed,
Enjoyed each other's company.

Alone With My Thoughts

Sitting alone, thinking of you.

Sitting by the water side,
My mind inside,
Open wide.

Water rippling in the stream,
Looking at what I see,
Beautiful
Is this real?
Or is it a dream?

Dream as if there is life forever,
Live as if there is only today.
Smile as though your heart will melt with feeling,
For our love will last forever and a day.

In this world we were meant for each other,
'You for me, and me for you,' as they say.
The time we spend is precious time together,
So we'll live, love, be happy, come what may.

Love's Rainbow

To love and be loved in return
Is a gift many yearn.
So keep looking and you will find
Love's rainbow,
You will not be left behind.

Love can be felt,
Love comes from within.
Love a cold heart can melt.
Love comes without sin.

Sow seeds of love and
Love you will reap.
Love is very strong,
Love is very deep.
Love can be a song
True love can
Forever keep.

Love

Love is free,
Free as a bird.
Love is like a song
That's good to be heard.

If you love someone,
You are rich without money,
As love cannot be bought
Like sugar, bread or honey.

Sugar is sweet, as you and I know,
All too soon its taste will go.
Love can stay forever,
Its flame can warm your soul,
Feelings, emotions, flowing
Forever to reach its goal.

So remember to give freely
The precious gift of love
To give is to receive as well
To gain and live to tell.

We know in life we reap
All that we do sow
Hold on, sow the seed of LOVE
Grow old with love,
Never let it go.

Zsu Zsu Zsu

Zsu zsu zsu zsuuu
Zsu zsu zsu zsu

What would I do without you
What would I do?
I could not live without you
What would I do?

You are my one desire
You hold me tight.
You're the one who lights the fire,
All through the night.

Zsu zsu zsu zsuuu
Zsu zsu zsu zsuuu.

My one and only true love

Feeling For You

When I look and see sadness in your eyes,
I think, 'why? Oh, why?'
What makes you think such deep thoughts
That take your smiles away?

Look around and you will see
That life is not such misery.
Changes come and go like the
Colours of the rainbow.
Some days are bright like colours of the
Beautiful sunlight,
Things look good, as they always should.

As life remains not the same,
Dull colours and sad days will for you pass away.
So be strong, carry on,
Go along with the flow,
Soon, your heart will surely know,
That someone loves you, someone cares,
Enough to make you smile again.
Then, my dear, you will see other days,
The sun will shine on you, again my love,
With your warm smile, and laughing eyes,
Your worries will melt right away.

To the Light of our Lives, Our Children

You shine like bright stars
Each one in their own way,
You are the reason we live,
Wake up each day.

Live your life to the full, my dears,
Your troubles be little,
Your worries be lost,
Your hopes be high,
Your dreams reach the sky.

Live for each other, my dears,
Then your strength will flow to and fro,
Life the meandering river does go,
As the river flows always to the sea,
Mingling and blending,
To become great with its unity,
So should you all, be big or small.

Our wish is there,
For each and all to love and share,
Then proud parents we will be,
To see our children living in
Grace and harmony.

To a Loved Lost Soul

Look into your heart my love,
You'll find I'm always there,
Search into your soul,
Look for the way.
There's still light enough for you,
To find the path you see,
The path that will lead you to me,
To us,
And our true destiny.

Till then I'll not say another word,
I'll not shed a tear,
I'll wait for you,
I'll ache for you,
Be it today, tomorrow
Or many a year.

Loving Can Hurt

You can sometimes hurt the one you love,
The one who cares, the one who shares,
It may not be intentionally,
But can still be there, so much there.
Words spoken hastily, without thought
Can strike like an arrow in the heart.
Tearing the love apart.
Love is strong and dear, don't fear,
It can keep together, and part us never,
Look upon this as a lesson learned,
And know for sure,
Love always has an open door.

Losing You

Losing you left me heartbroken,
My happy days are gone,
How will I carry on?
I am caught in a web,
I cannot get out,
How long will I scream and shout?

You went away and left me alone,
Why the sudden change of heart?
However could we be apart?

With your love I was like a rose in bloom,
Now I am withering and dying,
With no perfume.
Will the winds of change ever blow for me?
To bring you near
As for me my love, I'll always still be here.

But dream I will, and dream I do
That's the only way to keep hold of you.
I'll wait for you now till eternity, my love,
Lights will glow forever in my heart
For only you to see,
Till you are here, they'll shine for you
Show you the way to me,
Then forever you will stay,
Our love, again, could be.

Another day, another dream,
You're so far away, to touch, or see,
Another world, it seems.
I'm yearning for your love,
For you to hold me near,
With faith and hope I'll carry on,
My love for you will make me strong,
Of that I have no fear.

I will somehow get over this plight,
These days of darkness will turn into light,
Inside, my heart is ticking steadily,
With love that will last for eternity,
Then there'll be no tales of woe,
Come back to me, my love,
Give it another go.

No-one But You

No-one but you
Says the things that are right
No-one but you
Helps me make it through the night
When I am down and
Feeling so alone,
You are the one
Who's there to pick up the phone.

Your words are sincere
I wish you were near
You by my side,
Everything will be alright.

Wings of a Dove

If only I could fly away,
To have wings of a dove
Even just for a day.

There would be so much I would do
So much to see,
I would not be tied down,
I would be free.

So please let me loose,
Let me my own path choose,
I want to be my own man.
Live, love, laugh,
And do what I can.

Say The Words I Long To Hear

Time passes so slowly when you're not there,
Not to see you, not to share,
I feel so empty, so alone
My aching heart is like a heavy stone.
Come my love,
And say the words I long to hear.

You by my side,
My heart would glow,
I'd feel so happy
I'd want you to know
The world is mine.
If you'd be mine,
We'd live together
And part never
So please remember to say,
Your love is but a thought away.

I still think of you
So much each day,
Alas, each sigh, each tear,
For you my dear,
Is lost and washed away.

Let me not live another day,
Without your love, without your care,
Love is but a thought away.

Please say the words I long to hear,
I will love you forever.
I will need you now and always,
I want you always to be mine.

Left and Lonely

It's easy for you to tell me what to do,
You want me when you want,
And when you need me too.
Then you seem to change, act strange
Have a blinkered view.
Ignore me, as if I'm not there,
Shun me as if you don't care.

Let me tell you,
I am there, and I do care,
I have thoughts and feelings too,
Which I do try and share
With you.

My life is with you in it
And there is no other life.
I have not lived this long to start again,
So hear me when I say,
Keep me close to you,
Don't shun me away.
Let's start again, live again,
Save quarrels for another day.
And there is no other life,
I have not lived this long to start again,
So hear me when I say,

Keep me close to you,
Don't shun me away.
Let's start again, live again,
Save quarrels for another day.

Loving You

Loving you has been hard to do,
To always keep on the right track
Sometimes the road has not been easy
My love,
But never would I turn back.

Waiting

Like the falling of the last leaf off a great tree,
I'm left, barren of love, life, and beauty.

Alone I stand, nothing in my hand,
My heart full of sand.
Trickling away from me.
I wonder when this will end.
When will I be put out of this misery?

I can only hope and pray
That you'll again be mine someday.
My lonely life and troubled thought
Then will surely float away.
So,
My love,
If you come back to me,
And promise you will stay,
Then life will return to me,
I'll live and love many a day.
For you and I were meant to be.
And love can last till eternity.

Why, My Love?

Like a child with nowhere to go,
Nowhere to stay,
His heart turned to clay,
That's how I felt when you went away.
We drifted apart with no more to say.
But,
As a child's love is pure from the heart,
To give his all, not to take away.
That's how I'll be and how I'll stay.
Till you come back,
Forever and a day.

Our Children

Young blood,
One blood,
Pure blood,
Good blood.

Children of my heart's desire,
Fulfillers of our dreams,
Your true love will light my fires
On days when winter it seems.

You give your time, your thoughts so much,
I feel you're always near,
I feel that I am in touch,
Being alone, I have no fear.

Be forever young at heart,
For days soon come and go.
Make each day count for you,
See colours in every hue,
Mix all the shades, they are there for you,
Brighter, lighter, unique colours too.
Remember,
Take pride in whatever you do.

Paint your lives with one goal,
To achieve this, look into your souls,
Search for your dreams, look for your hopes,
See how you feel,
Make your dreams become real.

You oil the machine of life with your talent,
You give pleasure to all those who listen.
Your songs will live in their hearts forever,
The words will touch their soul,
As,
They are not empty words with holes.
They are words of might and meaning,
They are words straight from the heart,
They are words that should be heard apart.

This is the quality of life,
Love's golden thread will pull us together
May the precious twine break never.

May it grow stronger day by day,
Making memories as time passes,
Living, laughing, enjoying your way.

You love to sing and sing you do,
You sing the songs of love and life,
Live life to the full,
Dance and sing your songs,
As when you are happy,
Happiness spreads, people unite as one,

That gift is so special, that many do not have,
So carry on, making life a good game,
Remember,
We are on this Earth once,
Not time and time again.

Time

Time is so precious,
It waits for no man,
So let's be wise, and
Achieve what we can.
We're on this earth for such a short time.
So
Live life to the full,
Dear children of mine.

Your youth is not forever,
Your youth cannot be kept.
Your youth cannot be held in body or mind,
For sure,
It's always left behind.

Do not look back,
Cry and sigh,
But laugh and cheer, to the begotten years.
Look ahead to the future,
Seek your goal,
It will keep you going, it will keep you whole.
Be good people,
Try and gain,
Honour, self-respect.
And you will not have lived in vain.

So Near Yet So Far

As I sit and wonder
What I have left behind,
Words cannot say
Feelings do not show
Please show me the way
To let my love go.

Just enough to pass the time,
Just enough till we meet so
Till then, my love,
I am holding on
This is what I'd like you to know.

My love is so strong
My love is so deep
It keeps me awake
It lets me not sleep.

Still this is the way
To keep you in my heart
This is the way
So we shall never part.

Please Come Back

You took me to love's door,
Told me there to wait,
Suddenly, you turned back alone,
Left me at Heaven's gate.

You left me in a state of shock,
I was so confused,
As you were my rock.

You knew you meant the world to me,
You told me I did too,
We made precious memories,
You said your love was true.
With your love I'm still alive,
But, will I survive?
Can I survive?

Please tell me why.
Why again we didn't see the night sky?
The bright stars shining just for you and me,
Moonbeams dancing on the waves.
Was this futile? A fantasy?
All a dream?
Was our love never to be?
Our Heaven not meant for an eternity?

Look back, turn back,
Return to me,
Take me through love's door.
Take me through Heaven's gate,
You know how truly I love you.
Let's start our love anew.

Your Love is Like a Red Red Rose.

Gathering my memories like a bunch of flowers,
All full of beauty,
So many colours, perfume hues
Of whom do I prefer the best?
Which one outshines all the rest?
And reminds me of
The love I have for you.

I think of you, your love,
Like a red, red, rose,
It's the flower I hold so dear,
So vivid its colour, it always draws me near.
The perfume it gives so heavenly the scent,
As the day that I met you,
So "Heavenly meant".

To be with you is my only desire,
You are the one who sets my heart on fire.
You are the only one I want to live my life with
You are the only one to whom I'll give
All I can give.
Together we can and will sing love songs,
Gathering flowers,
Making life ours, and
Happy memories,
As we amble along.

One Unity

In life there's so much going on,
So much to do, so much to say
Living our busy lives each day,
Each in our individual way.
But hand on heart when we stop to think,
Of me to you, and you to me,
My love, my heart's desire,
We both share inside
One unity.

Remember Me

You take my breath away as I see you standing there,
I see the sun shining, lighting up your golden hair.
You looking at me, with your eyes so blue,
A brilliant blue, as the shimmering sea.
That's a part of why I love you
And what you mean to me.
You gaze back at me,
Deep into my soul, looking for my love,
We can feel that you and I are meant to be.

As precious seconds tick by,
It seems like eternity.
You know my heart is for you only,
I love the way you smile,
You can bring back joy, to me,
In my lonely life, my company,
That's the reason I want you to stay,
When I see you in this way.
BUT
Just then, the sun hid behind the clouds,
Took away its golden glow,
My heart stopped, my eyes dropped,
I looked at the time,
It was time for you to go.
Were we meant to be together

Only for this short while?
This memory will last for a lifetime.
So please remember me.
Get back to me,

Let's walk that extra mile.

Come Away With Me

Come away with me,
Come away just you and I
Come away my love,
Let the world pass us by.
Listen, and I'll tell you love,
I had a dream, it seemed so real,
That I was in a storm
No one else around me, nobody there.
Being twisted and turned,
Pulled here there and everywhere.
I could not see you or hold you close,
I was lost and blind in the world,
Dying like a wilting rose.
The sea was not blue for me,
The sky was not there
No colours of the rainbow,
Our love we could not share.
So lost and alone was I
Was I going to live?
Or was I fated to die?
Suddenly, I awoke, rubbed my eyes,
Sat up, and realised,
It was a dream, a nightmare,
A horrid lie.
We have a bond my love,
A true and everlasting tie.
I am glad to say,

My love for your was strong,
Enough to pull me through
I know where I belong,
May dreams like that never come true.

My Love in Flowers

Daffodils as yellow as the sun,
Elderberries making sweet wine to savour and have fun.
Snowdrops giving beauty on cold winter days,
Tulips like cups of nectar to drink and pledge to be mine always.
Irises the flowers of love, hope and promises that we are to be,
Narcissi staying strong, pure, like you are for me.
As my love,
You are a whole bouquet of flowers,
You are my destiny.

My Soulmate

You are the only one in my life,
You are my heart and soul,
You are the one that keeps me going,
With you, I am not a little piece,
I am whole.
I found my strength in my love for you
You are my soul mate, my best friend.
For you I'll keep on going,
Fighting the fight,
Doing what is right.
Till forever,
Till the end.

May the Rivers of Love Never Run Dry

No matter how far you are away from me
I know my love will last until eternity.
I keep you in my heart so you always seem near,
Keep you in my mind trying not to shed a tear.
Why did you have to go and leave me standing there
Was I not good enough for you?
For our true love to share?
Sometimes,
I try to forget the reason why you went,
I may be selfish, but can't forget the
Joyful, times we spent.
Then I have to stop and think,
Even though I truly love you
My dear, my friend, my love,
You are an individual too.
To live the life you choose, you have every right
In your heart there's the wish to help
Others in their plight.
Life comes one time around, you made your choice
You stood up to danger unknown
Let people hear your voice.
Good, my love, you are strong
Forgive me I am weak and wrong
So bless you and please carry on.
Fight the fight for what you believe in
Your sense of justice will not be deceiving.
As for me,

I'll regain faith which I nearly let go
I'll wait for you my love, that I want you to know,
We will laugh and love again
Cross the bridge of love you and I.
In our life dear heart,
May the rivers of love never run dry.

My Forsaken Love

You have the spirit of the winds, my love,
You wish to travel and sing your songs,
So be it,
Go where the winds will take you,
Go where your heart guides you,
Take what you have, carry it with care,
You know your talent lives inside you,
You believe, and yes, you achieve.
Your songs spread the message of love and humility,
Keep these assets, they will pull you along,
On the road to success,
That is where you really belong.
Your fate has flourished,
Your garden grown new shoots, nurture them,
Live, love, and always bind them,
But never forget your own roots.
Good luck to you my love,
Enjoy your travels far and wide,
I am here if ever you need me,
Just call my name and
I'll be right by your side.

My Special Love
My Sons

You have the **K**nowledge to follow your aspirations
Inspiration that will keep you going on
in life
Sunshine on your path to light the way
for you
Smiles on your journey to help you
make it through
Music in your soul that will last forever
Everlasting joy and harmony that will
keep our family together
True spirit that make You, YOU
unique diamonds.

Live for Today

There is no point in waiting,
Who knows what tomorrow brings?
Good news, bad news, all sorts of things.
Yesterday has been, never to return,
We can only remember,
And from what we can learn,
Change what we can,
Make better from the worse,
Then, my dear,
We would not have lived in vain,
We're here on this Earth, but once,
Not time and time again.

Life's journey has the same
Destination for us all,
Be we black, white, big, small, short, fat or tall.
Good soul, great values is what to aim for,
Pull together stand together, be at peace,
Not fight in war.

We are equal as they say, we have the same rights
Strive for better days and happy,
Contended nights.
Live for now and today,
Unite, clear the way, have fun,
Remember two are stronger than one.

A Fresh Start

To say you have no love
Is a crying shame,
To survive without love is hurtful,
To have no mark on someone,
No name.
Let your mind be free,
My dear then you will see,
Life is not such misery.

There is so much love around
Only to be searched for,
Just waiting to be found.
So,
Do not say you have no love,
Perhaps you may not see it,
Look inside deep, let go,
You will be able to feel it.
Have faith in your good self,
Do not be left on the shelf.

Happiness again will come to you
Run the run, have fun,
Start your life anew.

Beautiful Words

Dream as if there is life forever,
Live as there is only today.
Smile as though your heart will melt with feeling,
For our love will last forever and a day.

In this world we were meant for each other,
You for me, and me for you as they say,
The time we spend is precious time together,
We'll
Live, love, be happy, come what may.

Water for my Riverbed, You're Water for my Riverbed…

I once lived by a river
And basked in the bloom
The birds sang and chased each other til the evening loomed
But the river soon dwindled til just a trickle came
I tried to make out I didn't care but it just wasn't the same

My river turned to a desert
Where the sun, it burnt my soul
No protection from the pain
I had nowhere to go
I dreamt of my river, so colourful and flush
Now this floor cracked to the bed, fractured, crushed

But then a trickle, it returned and soon the water ran
Would the river return again and bring back my promised land?
Dare I dream a dream, that your love would then be mine
For a river without the water, is like a love left far behind.

Water for my riverbed, you're water for my riverbed…

Ron

This poem was written by my son Ron, and I love it so much I wanted to include it in my book.

ND - #0273 - 080726 - C0 - 216/138/5 - PB - 9781780354750 - Gloss Lamination